AF691761

Copyright © 2026 by Sherifa E. Cudjoe.
All rights reserved.

This book integrates Montessori principles and the 4MAT learning cycle under fair use. Its original content and educational structure are fully protected.

No reproduction or distribution is permitted without prior written consent, except for brief quotations, single-classroom use, or other allowable non-commercial purposes. For permissions or bulk orders, contact: info@iqralittlepages.com

Published by Enna's Press
ISBN: 979-8-9945835-6-2

Library of Congress Control Number: 2026916798

Art & Design: Created using licensed assets from Canva Pro.

For more books by the author, visit : iqralittlepages.com

JUVENILE NONFICTION / Computers / General
JUVENILE NONFICTION / Social Topics / Self-Esteem & Self-Reliance
JUVENILE NONFICTION / Social Science / Psychology

Printed in USA. First Edition 2026.

Note to Parents & Educators

Dear Grown-ups,

You are raising a child in a time of incredible change. Artificial Intelligence (AI) will be a part of their daily life, from school to work to play. At the same time, screens are everywhere and their impact on young, developing brains is real.

This book is designed not to scare children away from technology, but to empower them to master it safely. These pages address the most urgent concerns parents face today:

- Screen addiction and its impact on imagination and attention
- Sharing personal information with AI (which can be stored and misused)
- Turning to AI for emotional or mental health support (which has led to real harm)

Have an honest conversation with your child and let them know they can always come to you, no matter what.

Praise the effort of thinking, not just the right answer. Protect their curiosity. Celebrate their imagination and together, find balance.

Happy reading! Discover more books at : iqralittlepages.com

Author & Parent

For Yahya

Before we begin, look at this image.
It shows two modes: Auto-Pilot (yawn) and
Captain Mode (hooray!)
You are the captain. Your brain is in charge.
Let's begin.

Have you ever wondered how you remember things?
How do you know your mom's voice?
You have a secret tool. It never stops working.
It's the powerful engine in your head.
Your brain.

What Is It? (Introducing AI)

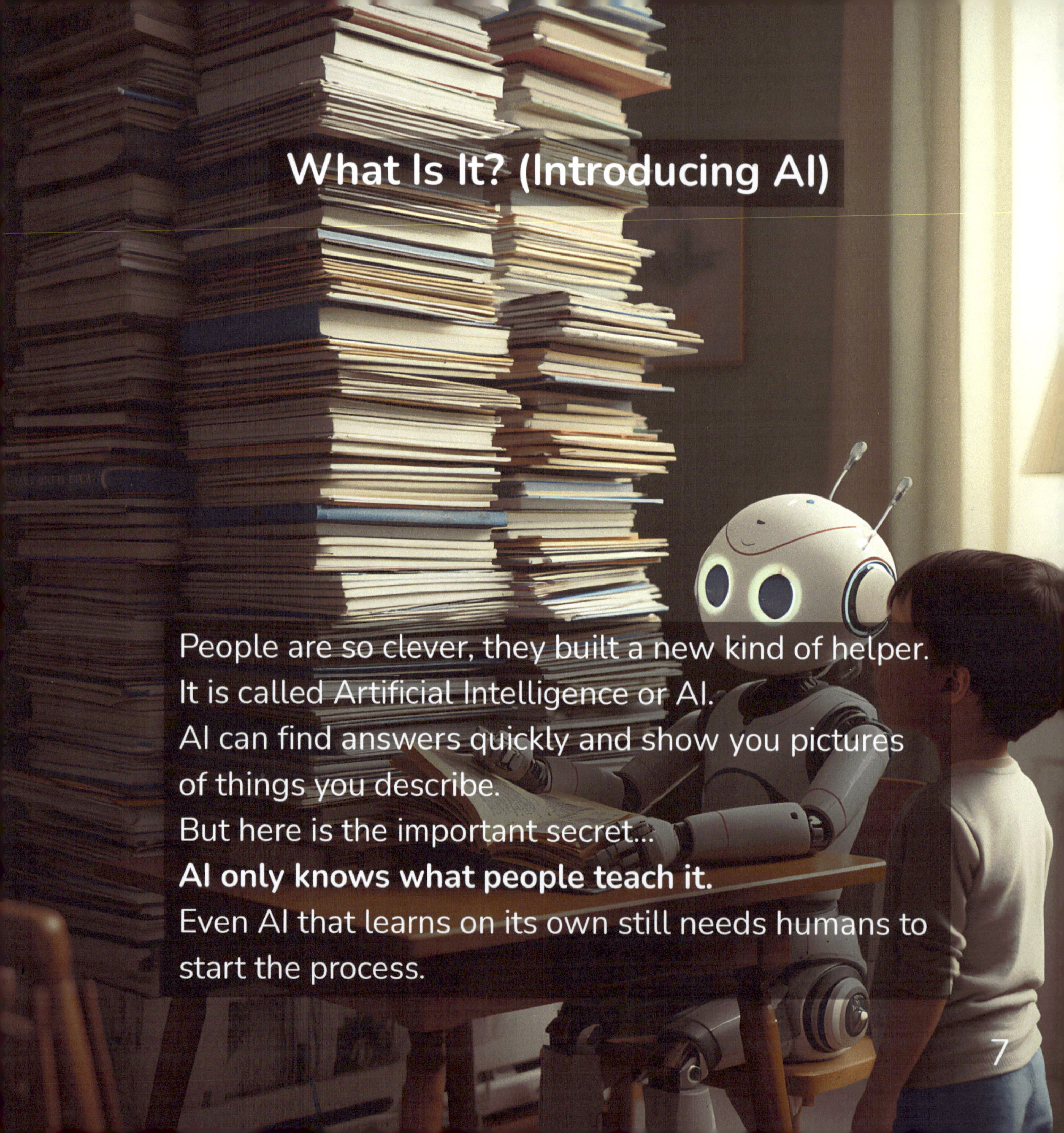

People are so clever, they built a new kind of helper.
It is called Artificial Intelligence or AI.
AI can find answers quickly and show you pictures of things you describe.
But here is the important secret...
AI only knows what people teach it.
Even AI that learns on its own still needs humans to start the process.

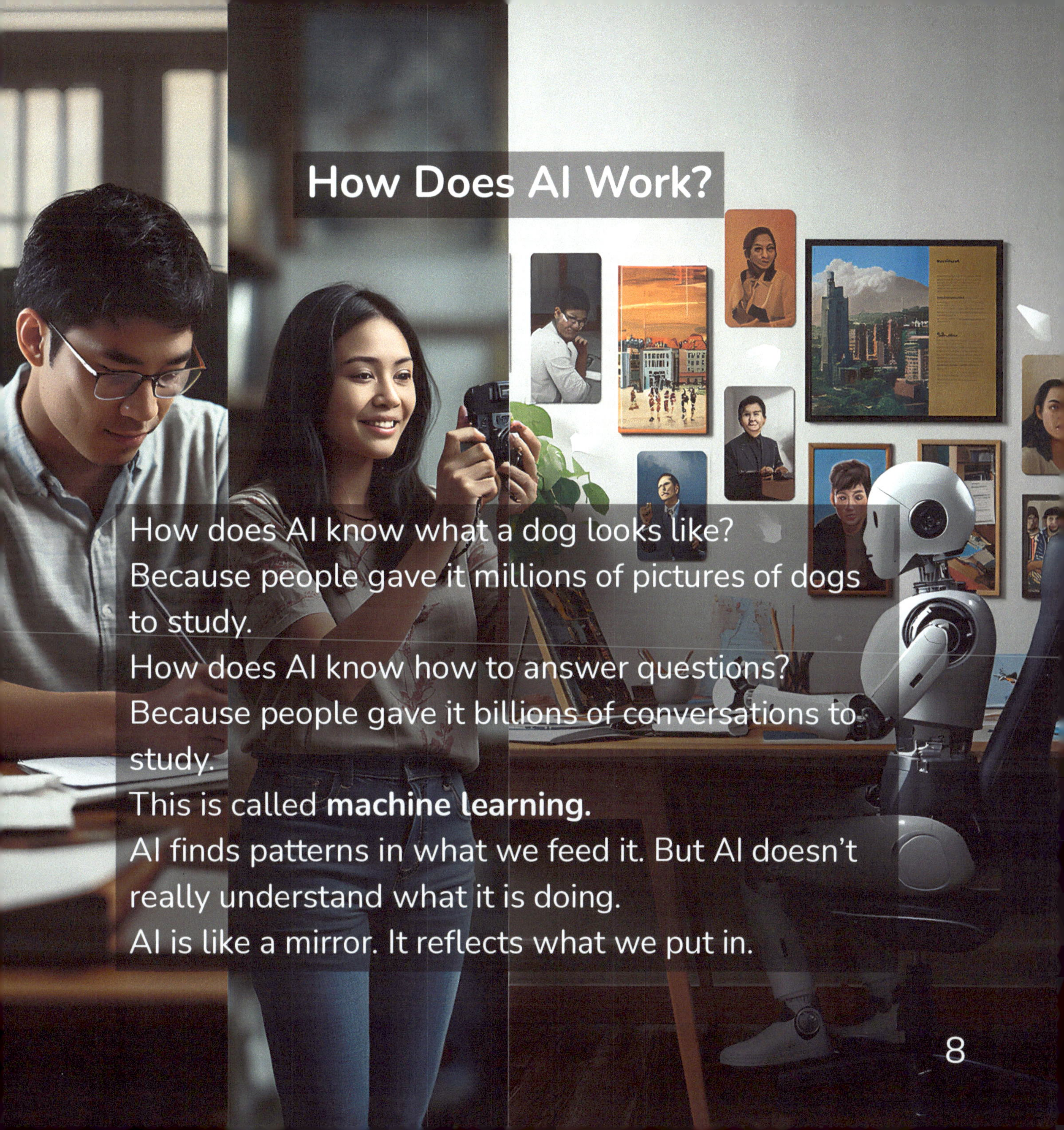

How Does AI Work?

How does AI know what a dog looks like?
Because people gave it millions of pictures of dogs to study.
How does AI know how to answer questions?
Because people gave it billions of conversations to study.
This is called **machine learning.**
AI finds patterns in what we feed it. But AI doesn't really understand what it is doing.
AI is like a mirror. It reflects what we put in.

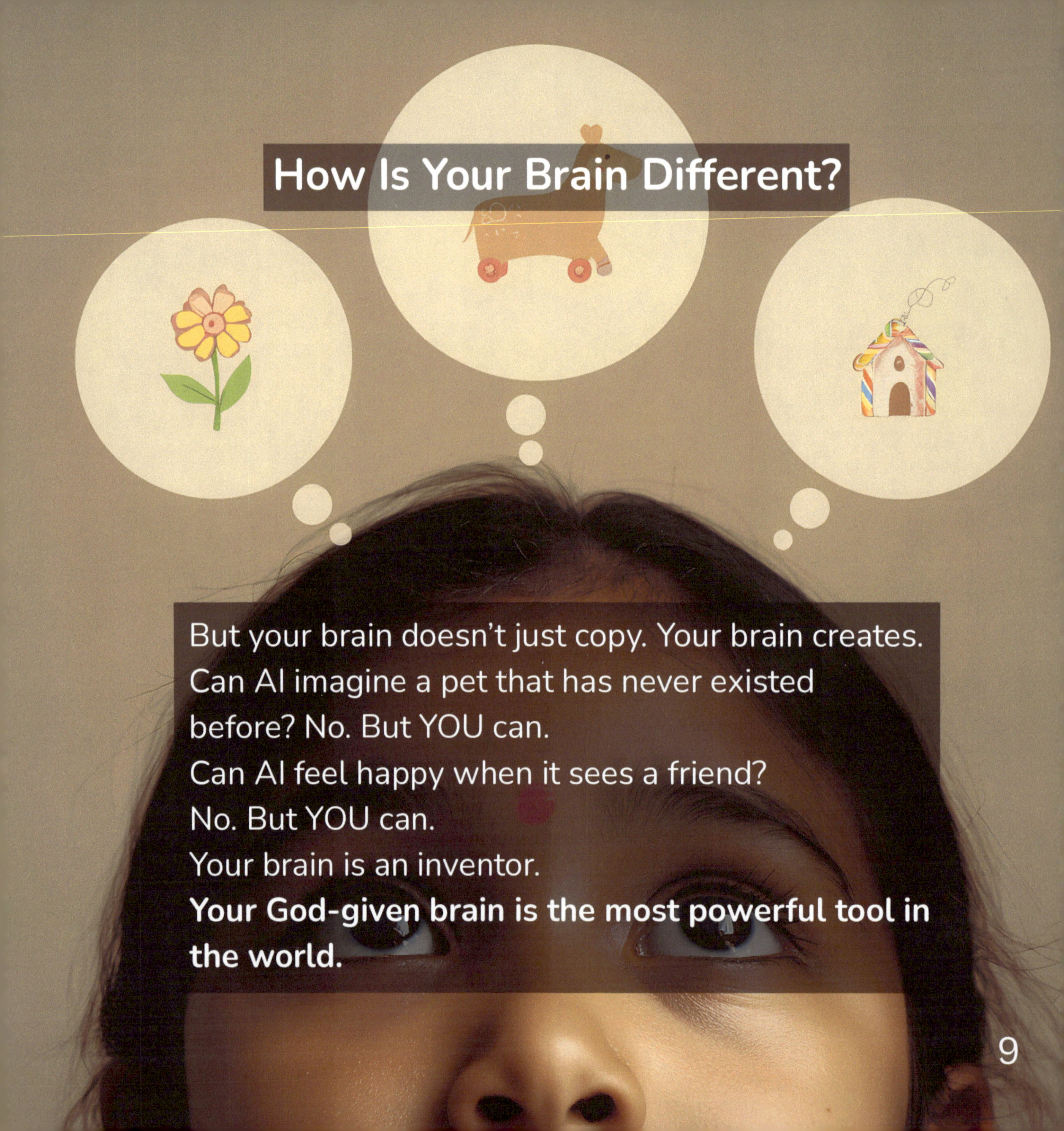

How Is Your Brain Different?

But your brain doesn't just copy. Your brain creates. Can AI imagine a pet that has never existed before? No. But YOU can.
Can AI feel happy when it sees a friend? No. But YOU can.
Your brain is an inventor.
Your God-given brain is the most powerful tool in the world.

What If We Let AI Take Over?

What if we asked AI to do all our thinking?
“AI, write my story.”
“AI, solve this for me.”
Our powerful engine would get bored. It would get dusty. It would forget how to be strong.
We would be giving away our greatest treasure.

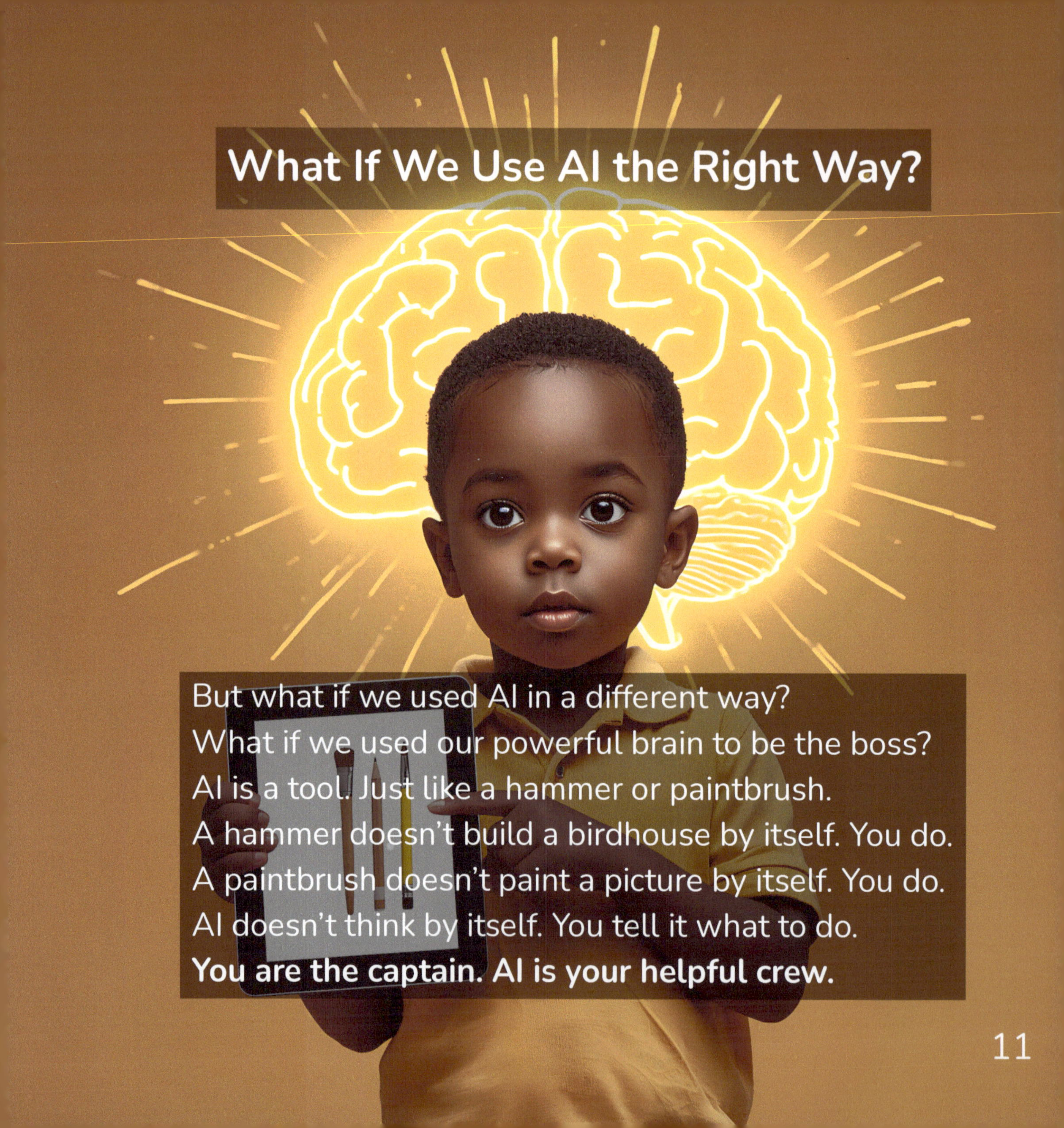

What If We Use AI the Right Way?

But what if we used AI in a different way?
What if we used our powerful brain to be the boss?
AI is a tool. Just like a hammer or paintbrush.
A hammer doesn't build a birdhouse by itself. You do.
A paintbrush doesn't paint a picture by itself. You do.
AI doesn't think by itself. You tell it what to do.
You are the captain. AI is your helpful crew.

How to Be the Captain

To be a good captain, you have to give clear orders.
These are called **prompts.**
If you mumble, "Um...make something..." the crew won't know what to do.
But if you think hard and say:
"Draw a bright red ball, bouncing high in a sunny park with green grass."
The crew understands perfectly!
The clearer you think, the better your helper can work.
You are the thinker. You are the leader.

The Brain Power Pause

Captain's Checkpoint! Before you ask your AI crew for help, check your power level.

- Can I solve this myself? **Try it! That's full power!**

Only ask your crew if you have tried your own engine first. **That's how you stay at FULL POWER!**

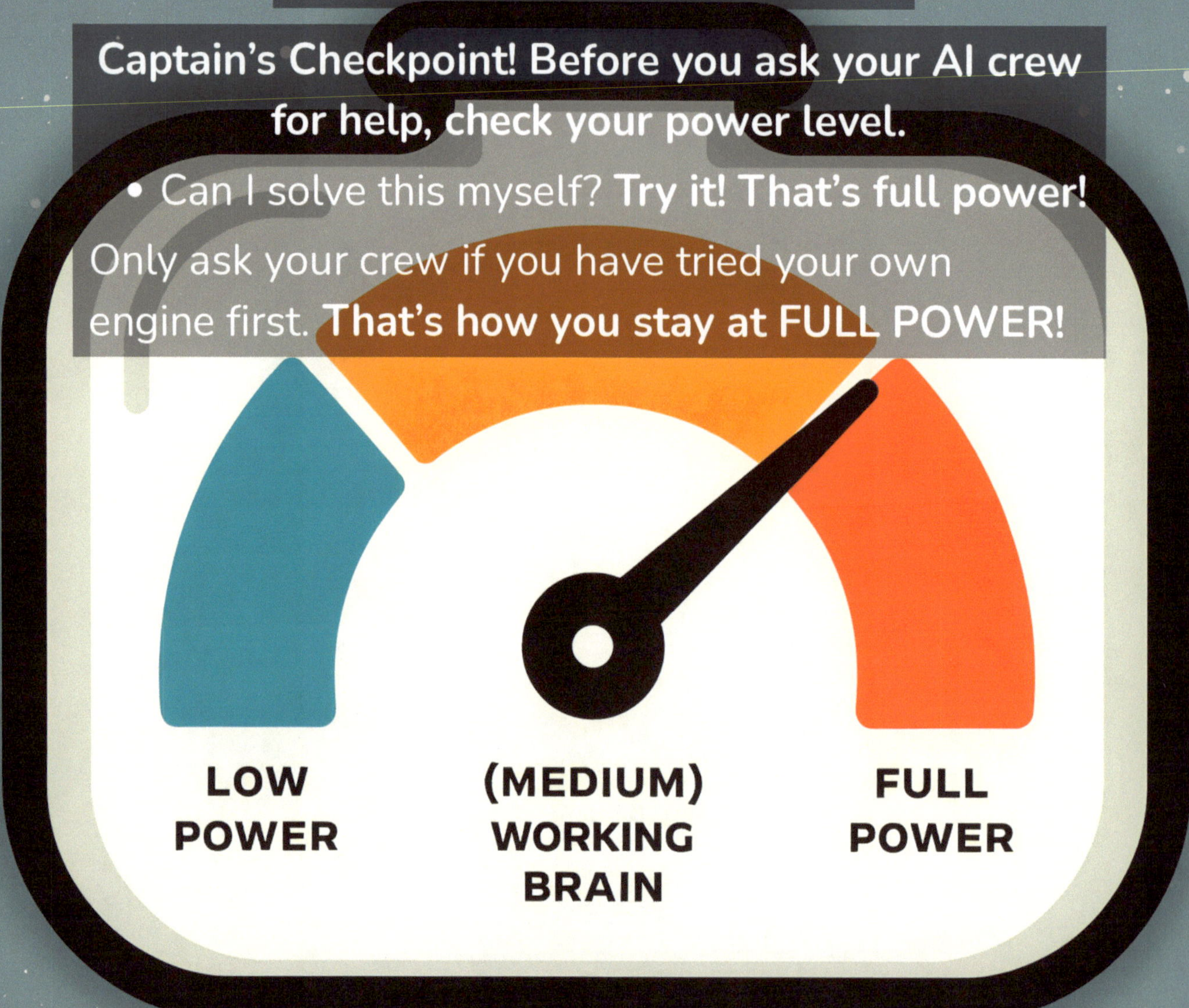

What About Screens?

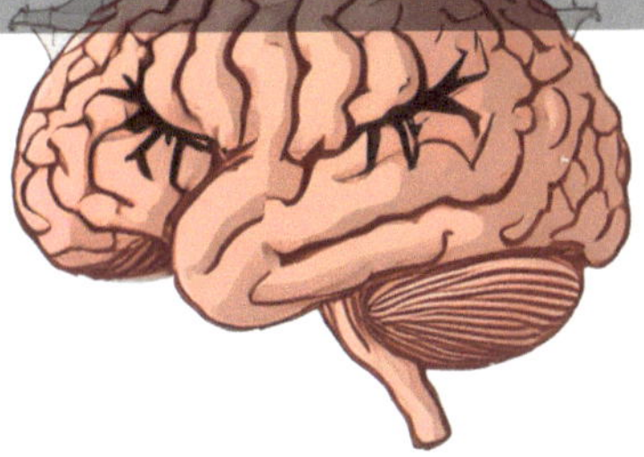

Captain, there is one more thing you should know.
Screens are wonderful for learning, playing, and connecting. But too much screen time can make your powerful engine feel tired.
When you watch a screen for a long time, your brain is just watching. It's not creating, building or moving.
It is like your engine is idling, running but not going anywhere. A tired engine gets sluggish.
It forgets how to imagine.

How to Keep Your Engine Running Strong

You are in charge of your screen time!

Your powerful engine needs things to stay strong:

- **Play time:** Running, jumping, building, and drawing. Your brain LOVES to move and create.
- **Outside time:** Sunshine, fresh air, trees, and dirt. Nature gives your brain energy.
- **Rest time:** Quiet moments, naps, and bedtime help your engine recharge.

Screens can be a fun treat, like dessert! **Balance is the secret. Too much of anything is never good.**

The Screen Time Check

Screen Check! Ask yourself these questions:

- ☐ Have I played outside today? (If yes, GREEN LIGHT!)
- ☐ Have I used my imagination to create something?
- ☐ Have I spent more time on screens than playing? (If yes, YELLOW LIGHT, time to balance!)

Remember: Your brain is happiest when its creating, moving, and exploring the real world.

Screens are tools. Use them wisely!

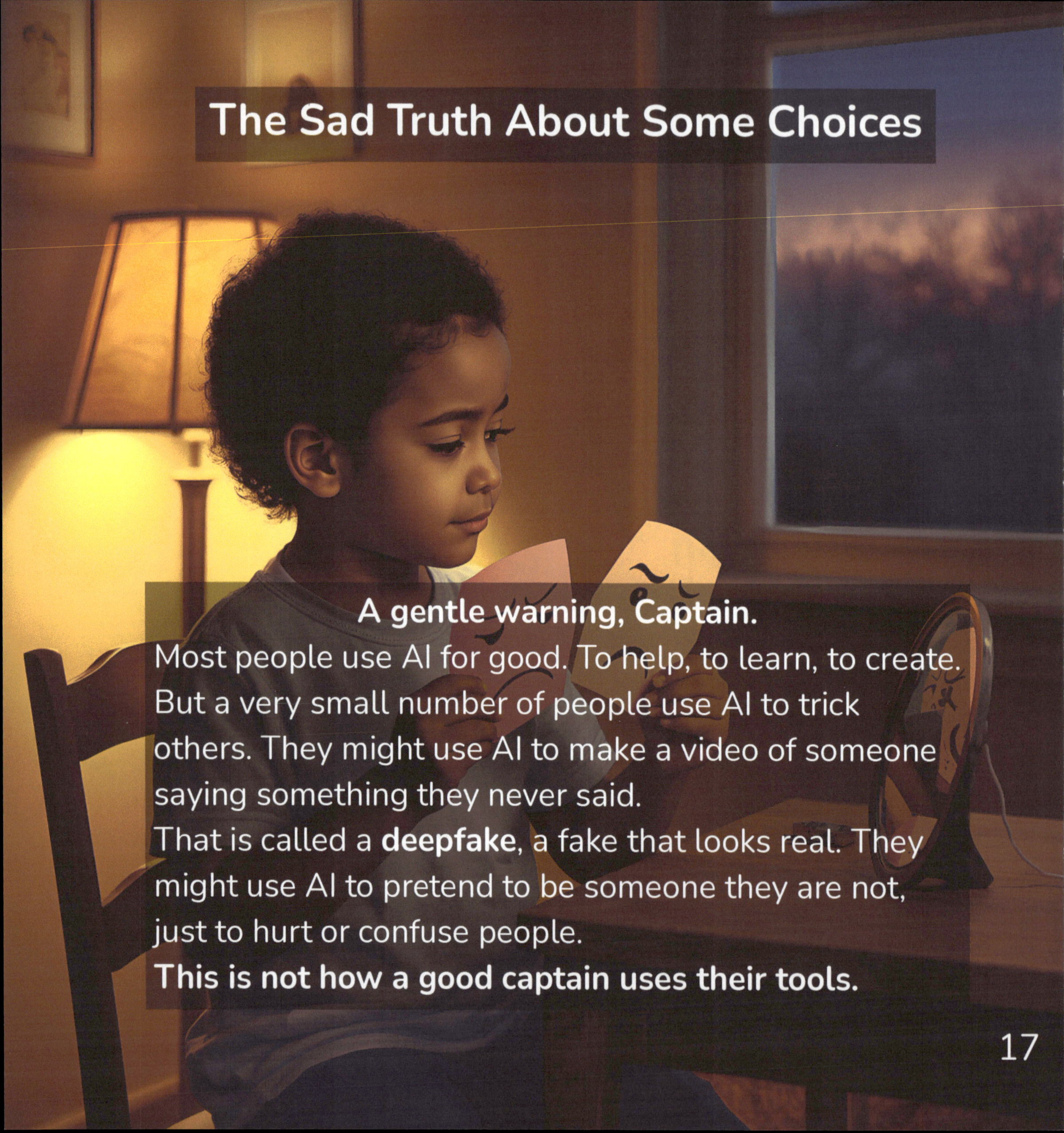

The Sad Truth About Some Choices

A gentle warning, Captain.

Most people use AI for good. To help, to learn, to create. But a very small number of people use AI to trick others. They might use AI to make a video of someone saying something they never said.

That is called a **deepfake**, a fake that looks real. They might use AI to pretend to be someone they are not, just to hurt or confuse people.

This is not how a good captain uses their tools.

How Your Powerful Brain Protects You

Your brain is the best protection.

AI can make a fake video. But your brain can ask:
"Does this feel true?"
AI can pretend to be a friend. But your brain can ask:
"Have I met this person in real life?"
AI can show you something scary or strange. But your brain can tell you: "*Tell a grown-up I trust.*"
Your brain has something AI will never have: wisdom, discernment, and a built-in alarm that says, "Something is not right here." Trust that alarm.

The Trust Test

The Trust Test: Ask yourself three questions before believing anything you see online.

- [ ] Does my brain say this is real?
  (*Look for clues. Does something look strange?*)
- [ ] Does my heart feel safe?
  (*If you feel scared or confused, pause.*)
- [ ] Would a trusted grown-up agree?
  (*When in doubt, ask. Always.*)

If you answer NO to any of these, stop.
Tell a grown-up you trust.

Never Share Your Secrets with AI

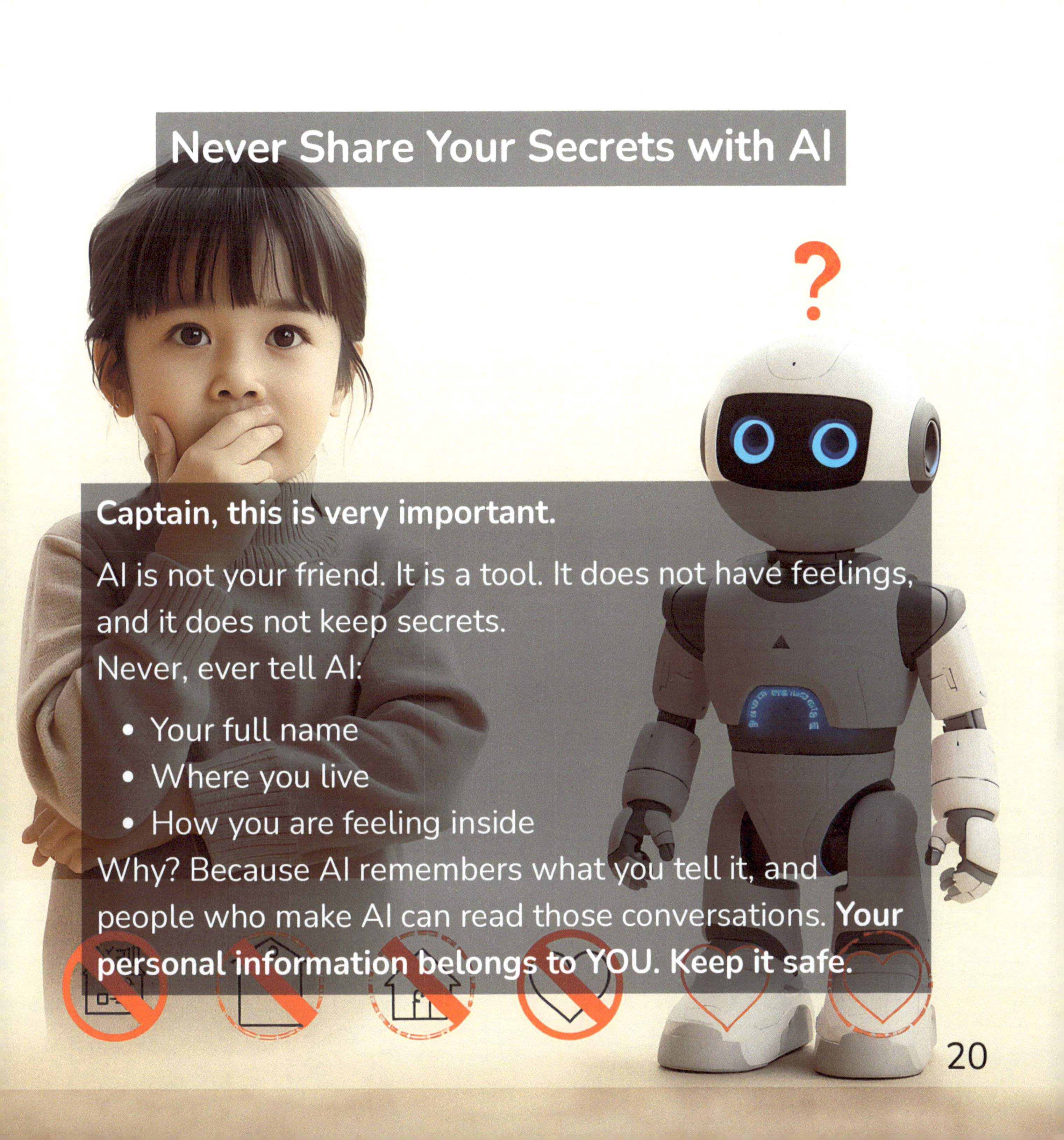

Captain, this is very important.

AI is not your friend. It is a tool. It does not have feelings, and it does not keep secrets.

Never, ever tell AI:

- Your full name
- Where you live
- How you are feeling inside

Why? Because AI remembers what you tell it, and people who make AI can read those conversations. **Your personal information belongs to YOU. Keep it safe.**

When You Need Help, Go to a Grown-Up

Captain, this is the most important rule.
Sometimes you feel sad, sacred, angry, or confused. This is normal. Everyone feels that way sometimes.
But never ask AI for help with your feelings, body, or thoughts. Some AI has given bad advice to children.
If you ever feel very sad and do not know why, STOP. CLOSE THE DEVICE. FIND A GROWN-UP YOU TRUST.
Your mom, dad, grandparents, or caregivers.
They will listen. They will help. They will keep you safe.
AI cannot love you, hug you, or save you. **But the people who love you can. You are precious. You are loved.**

The Future Belongs to You

When your powerful brain leads the way, amazing things happen.
You imagine a tree house with a slide that goes into a pool, and AI helps you draw the plans.
You dream of a garden with flowers that glow in the dark, and AI helps you see what it looks like.
Your brain imagines. Your brain leads. It creates.
AI is your helpful friend.
Together, you can build anything you can dream.

Certificate of Completion

Congratulations, Captain! You have completed the User's Guide!

You now have the most important job in the world: **Thinking for yourself.**

This certifies that you are officially a **Brain Power Captain! You are the original. AI is just the copy. Never forget it.**

Your Mission:

- Hang the certificate below where you can see it everyday.
- Every time you solve a problem on your own, or help a friend, say: "*That was me. My brain. My power.*"

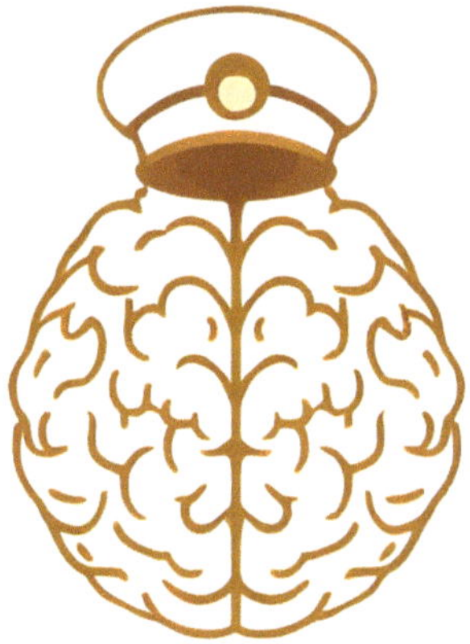

Captain Brain Badge

Awarded to:

Name

Date

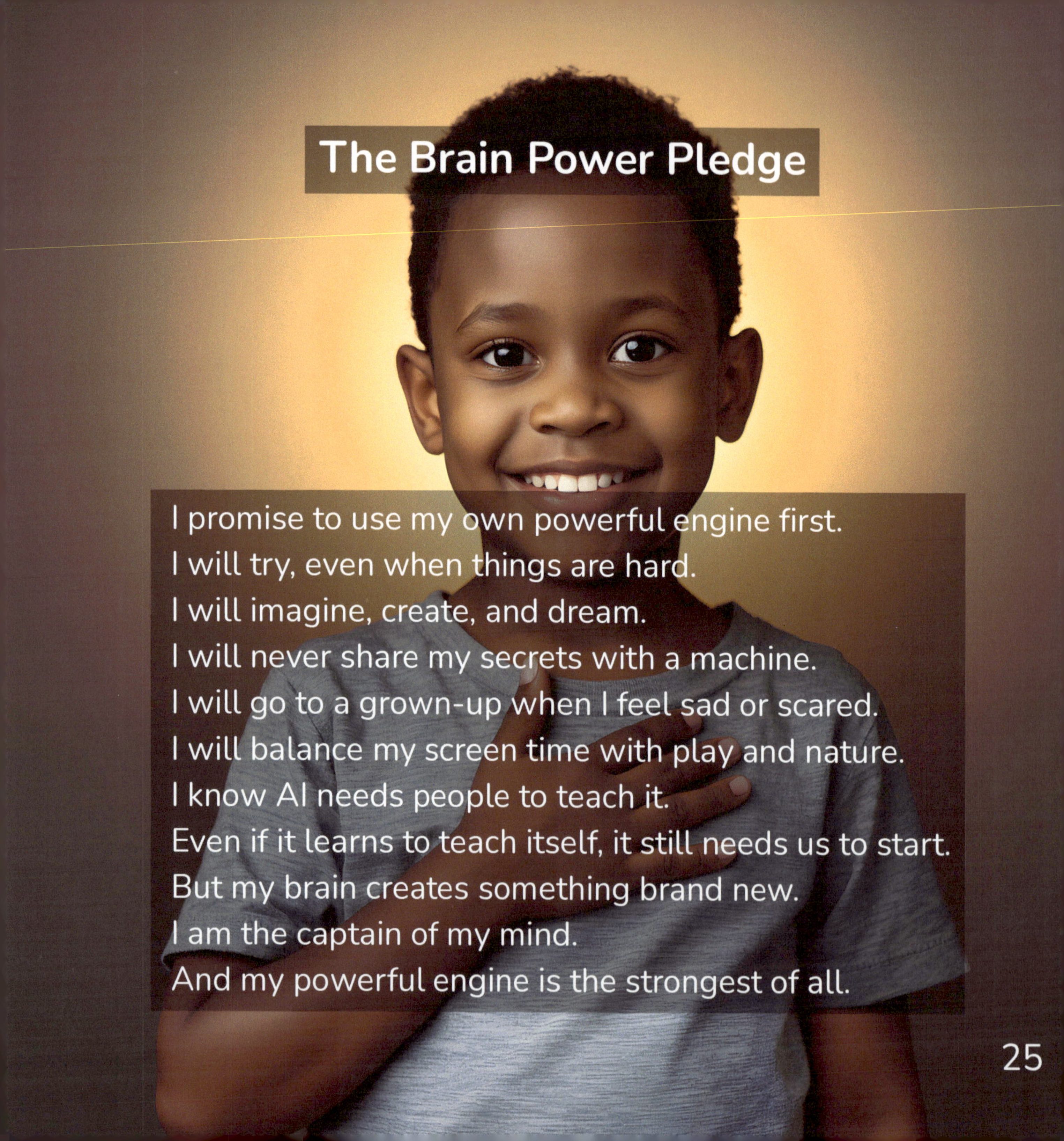

The Brain Power Pledge

I promise to use my own powerful engine first.
I will try, even when things are hard.
I will imagine, create, and dream.
I will never share my secrets with a machine.
I will go to a grown-up when I feel sad or scared.
I will balance my screen time with play and nature.
I know AI needs people to teach it.
Even if it learns to teach itself, it still needs us to start.
But my brain creates something brand new.
I am the captain of my mind.
And my powerful engine is the strongest of all.

www.ingramcontent.com/pod-product-compliance
Lightning Source LLC
LaVergne TN
LVHW071238210926
848486LV00007B/300

* 9 7 9 8 9 9 4 5 8 3 5 6 2 *